G is for Grace,
and so is this book
S. N.

L is for Leslie,
my lovely historian
N. B.

The Church History ABCs: Augustine and Twenty-five Other Heroes of the Faith
Copyright ©2010 by Stephen J. Nichols and Ned Bustard
Published by Crossway
    1300 Crescent Street
    Wheaton, Illinois 60187

Book design and illustration: Ned Bustard
First printing 2010
Printed in China

Hardcover ISBN: 978-1-4335-1472-2
PDF ISBN: 978-1-4335-1473-9
Mobipocket ISBN: 978-1-4335-1474-6
EPub ISBN: 978-1-4335-2466-0

Library of Congress Cataloging-in-Publication Data
Nichols, Stephen J., 1970-
  The church history ABCs : Augustine and 25 other heroes of the faith / Stephen J. Nichols, Ned Bustard.
     p. cm.
  ISBN 978-1-4335-1472-2 (hc)
  1. Christian biography--Juvenile literature. 2. Church history--Juvenile literature. 3. English language--Alphabet--Juvenile literature. I. Bustard, Ned. II. Title.
  BR1704.N53 2010
  270.092'2--dc22   2009043263

Crossway is a publishing ministry of Good News Publishers.

RRD   26   25   24   23
16   15   14   13   12   11   10   9   8

STEPHEN J. NICHOLS

NED BUSTARD

the **Church History**

ABCs

Augustine and 25 Other Heroes of the Faith

CROSSWAY

WHEATON, ILLINOIS

INTRODUCTION

You probably enjoy hearing stories of your parents or grandparents. Of course, everybody walked to school back then and it was always snowing! You even like to hear stories about your friends. You know, like the time Jack fell off the boat and got all wet.

You enjoy these stories because the people in them are very special to you. You also like these stories because these stories tell you something about you.

The people of church history are also very special to you. Their story is your story. Their story also tells you something about you. The Bible tells us that we all belong to one big family, the family of God. And there are a lot of stories to be told in this big family. In this book, we can only tell the story of twenty-six of these people because there are only twenty-six letters in our alphabet. But there are many more stories that could be told.

In fact, this story hasn't even ended yet. Someday you will be adding your own story to it.

So open these pages and meet your new friends. They all have a great story to tell. . . .

When I was a young boy, I took some pears that did not belong to me. I did not want the pears; I just enjoyed doing wrong. But God loved me and Christ died to forgive all my sin. Years later when I was serving as a bishop, I wrote two famous books. And I worked hard to remind the church that God loves us before we love him.

A is for
apricot, apple,
and **Augustine**
—Africa's ancient bishop

SAINT AUGUSTINE

B is for boat, berries, and Anne **Bradstreet,** America's first bard

I was born in England. I would spend my days reading books, especially poetry. Because we weren't free to practice our faith, we boarded a large boat bound for Boston. My father was the governor of the colony and later my husband was, too. We had a very busy house. At night when it was quiet I would write my poetry. I wrote about kings and queens and nature and about my family. I also wrote about trusting God even during hard times—like when my house burned down. They call me a "bard." That is a fancy word for "poet." I just wanted to use my gift to serve and glorify God.

ANNE BRADSTREET

JOHN CALVIN

C is for catfish, castle, and John **Calvin,** champion Reformer

I grew up in France and went to college in Paris, a big city with big cathedrals. I was only 14, and I was not very interested in church or in God. Then God captured my heart and made me his child. I left France for Switzerland—but I never learned to yodel. I ended up at the city of Geneva. I taught people all about God's creation, all about Christ's death on the cross, and all about becoming good and caring citizens. We sent missionaries across the border into France and even across the seas to Brazil. I wrote many books. In one of them I chimed, "Every blade of grass and every color in this world is intended to make us rejoice in God."

JOHN DONNE

I lived in England during the time of the Reformation. England is a really big island. I once said, "No man is an island." We all depend on each other. I went to Cambridge for study, but I spent most of my time outdoors writing poetry. Then I moved to London. I would walk across the bridges at night and write even more poems. During the day, I was a lawyer and was soon elected a member of Parliament. Finally, when I was forty-five years old I became a pastor. My wife and I had a dozen—that's twelve—kids. People like to read my poems, saying they're quite dramatic. My favorite poems were my *Devotions*. In one of them I said, "Don't ask for whom the bell tolls, it tolls for thee."

D is for door, drawing, and John **Donne**

E is for eggs, elephants, and Jonathan **Edwards**

I was the only brother to ten sisters. They helped me with my studies and taught me to ride horses. I started pinning scraps of cloth to my coat to help me remember ideas I would get on long horseback rides. I used these ideas in sermons I preached and in books I wrote. With my friend George Whitefield, I was part of the Great Awakening in the American colonies. I was also a missionary to the Mohican Indians. And for a little while I was even president of Princeton University. Everywhere I went I wanted people to enjoy God and to enjoy what God has made—even spiders.

JONATHAN EDWARDS

9

F is for frog, fire, and John **Foxe,** writer of heroes of the faith

I was a teacher on a big estate where they had fox hunts and grand feasts. But then Queen Mary came to the throne in England. She put many Christians in jail. I was forced to leave the country with my wife and sailed across the English Channel. Back in England, many of my friends were put to death for their faith. I wrote a book about these heroes of the faith.

The book's title is really long, so folks just call it *Foxe's Book of Martyrs.* These were brave people who went through many cruel and scary punishments. They all had faith in a great God. I returned to England when Elizabeth I came to the throne. I was so grateful, I dedicated my book to her.

JOHN FOXE

JANE GREY

G is for
garden, gown,
and Lady Jane **Grey,**
queen for nine days

When I was just a little girl I taught myself Greek and Hebrew. I used to write letters to the Reformers like Ulrich Zwingli (skip ahead to "Z" and you'll see). I was a great niece to King Henry VIII. His son, Edward VI, was the next king. A very godly king, Edward VI died after just a few years on the throne. Since I was part of the Reformation, I was put on the throne as England's queen. I only lasted nine days until— Mary's army marched through the gates. Then I was put in the Tower of London. Just before I died as a martyr, I gave my sister my Bible. Inside it I wrote, "Rejoice in Christ, as I do. Follow the steps of your master Christ, and take up your cross."

HIPPOLYTUS

H is for
hopscotch, hot dog, and **Hippolytus**

Hi. Let's get one thing straight, my name is Hippo*lytus*, not hippo*potamus*—that's a very big animal with really short legs. I'm not Hippocrates, either—he was the father of medicine. And I'm not a hippocampus—that's a make-believe horse with a fish tail. Nope, I'm Hippolytus. I lived in Rome

around AD 200, and I wrote many books. One of them was *The Refutation of All Heresies*. A heresy is a false teaching, and some of these false teachings denied the humanity of Jesus. Look across the page to see what my friend Ignatius has to say about that. I never signed my name to my books and soon people forgot all about me. However, in the 1840s they found a statue of me. On it was a list of all the books I wrote. Now you know who I am and you know that H is for Hippolytus.

A long, long time ago, in a place far, far away . . . I always wanted to say that. It is true, though, I was born before anyone else in this whole book. I was a pastor in Antioch, the city where we were first called Christians. Like the apostles (and I knew at least one of them), I would write letters to churches. During my time, some people were teaching false ideas about Christ. I reminded them that Christ came down from heaven. We call this the *incarnation*—a long and fancy word that also starts with an I. It means that Christ, who is God, became human just like us. He was born as a baby and grew up and played as a boy. Jesus was just like us so he could die for us on the cross. I took a great stand for my beliefs and was sent to Rome as a prisoner, where I was martyred by being eaten by lions.

IGNATIUS

13

J is for Jupiter, jelly beans, and Absalom **Jones's** journey to freedom

I was born a slave and worked in the fields. But I wanted to be free. When I was ten, I was sent to work in a grocery store in Philadelphia, the home of the Liberty Bell. I worked very hard at my job and went to school at night. Later on I married and we saved enough money to buy our freedom. At church one Sunday they told us to sit in a certain place because of the color of our skin. We left and formed a new church, and I soon became the pastor. At our new church I preached that God was the father of us all, red and yellow, black and white. Our church was its own Liberty Bell, ringing out a message of freedom for everyone.

ABSALOM JONES

JOHN KNOX

Knox Knox!

Who's there?

My last name starts with a silent K, but I refused to keep silent! The church in my home of Scotland wasn't following the Bible, and neither were the kings and queens. So I spoke up. I was arrested and put on a galley ship. Then they kicked me out of the country, so I went to see my friend John Calvin. Later I went back home and kept on preaching and writing. The gospel spread all around the kingdom. I kept busy and even helped start the Presbyterian church, too.

K is for kirk, king, and John **Knox**

15

MARTIN LUTHER

I saw the whole world change in my lifetime, and I had a little something to do with it. I helped the church find its way back to the Bible and back to Christ and his work on the cross. It all started when I hammered a piece of paper to the church door at Wittenberg in Germany. Now don't try that at your church. People don't like that. In fact, it turned out that the Pope didn't like it and they put me on trial in Worms (the city called Worms—not the things crawling in the ground). But I stood up for the Word of God. The Reformation spread all around Germany and soon all around Europe. I loved to preach and teach. I always enjoyed eating and good music. But most of all I loved to teach children the catechism. Even our family dog would listen in.

L is for lollipop, lute, and Martin **Luther,** larger-than-life Reformer

. . . take one down, pass it around, **95 Theses** on the church door . . .

M is for muffin, moose, and **Monica,** mother of Augustine

I'm Monica, and my son is back on the first page. I loved Augustine very much and prayed for him every day. I kept a close watch on that boy of mine. When he moved, I followed close behind. We even made it all the way to Milan, Italy. There he met a great pastor, Bishop Ambrose, and a great friend, Alypius. Eventually, my son met our mighty God. I was so happy when Augustine told me that he had become a follower of Jesus. That's what matters most, and that's a mom's mission.

MONICA

17

N is for noodles, nachos, and John **Newton,** writer of "Amazing Grace"

A - maz-i
'Twas grace
Thro' man
When we'v

"I was blind, but now I see." That's a line I wrote in the song "Amazing Grace." But it took me a long time to learn that. My father built ships and I first went to sea at age eleven. Later, I became captain of my own ship. But I used my ship to trade slaves. I could not see God's grace or God's love for me. I was blinded by my sin. After a bad storm and a shipwreck I cried out to God for help. He helped me and he saved me from my sin. I spent the rest of my life preaching, writing hymns, and working very hard to put an end to the slave trade. God's grace is amazing.

JOHN NEWTON

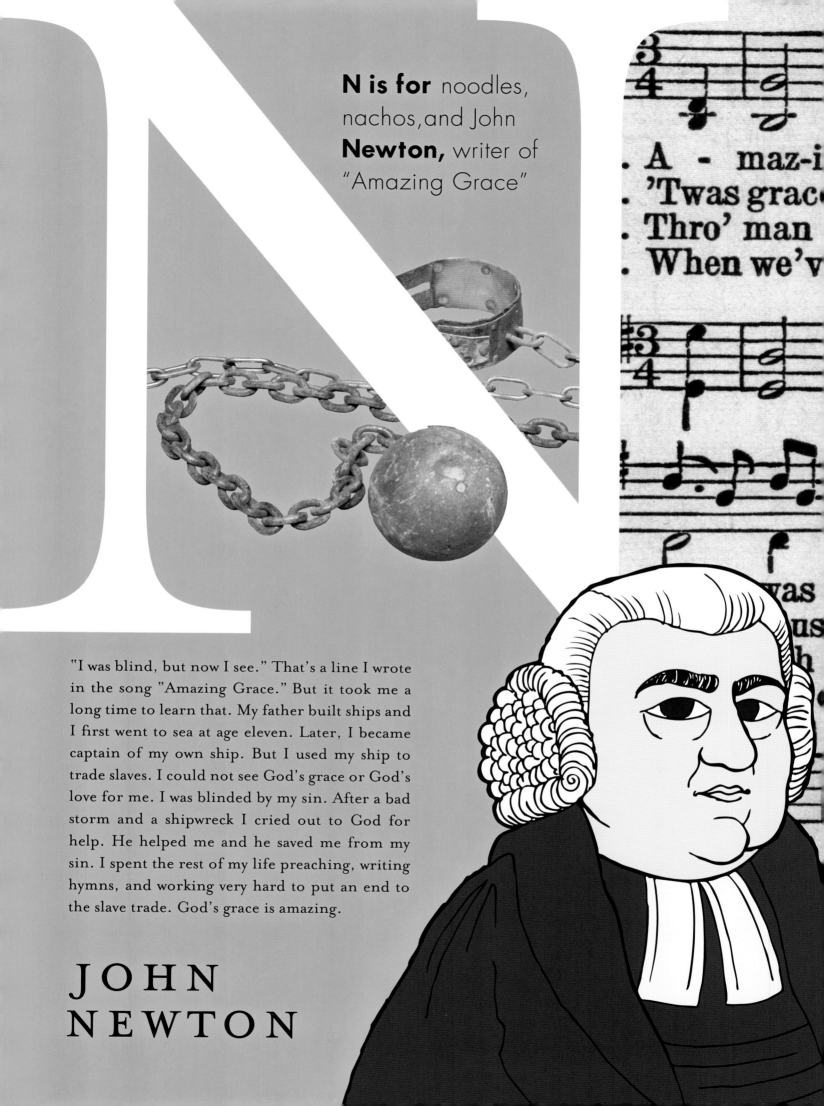

DOMI
NUS
ILLV
ME

O is for

octopus, orange,
and John **Owen,**
Oxford Reformer

I grew up outside of Oxford in England. When I got a little older I went there for college. I played the flute and I liked sports. I threw the javelin and ran the long jump. I also cracked open the books. Later I moved to London. England was in a civil war back then. It was a dangerous time. After the war, I went back to Oxford. I wrote many books. Some were really loooong. Even though I liked sports, I realized we don't have the power within ourselves to do what God requires. God works in us. One of my many friends was John Bunyan. He showed me a copy of something he wrote. I said, "John, you have to publish this." He did. It's called *Pilgrim's Progress.* That book title has two P's in it. And "P" is our next letter.

PATRICK

P is for pirates, potatoes, and **Patrick**—patron saint of Ireland

The stories many people tell about me are filled with snakes and shamrocks, but when I told people about my life I wrote, *"I am Patrick, yes a sinner and simplest of peasants."* When I first went to Ireland, I was sixteen years old. But I hadn't been planning on going there—I was captured by pirates! They sold me to the Irish, who put me to work herding sheep. I prayed a lot. Finally, I escaped and sailed back home to England. There I studied to be a priest and later went back to Ireland. The people were in spiritual darkness and needed someone to preach the gospel to them. I prayed for Christ to protect me and for God's purpose to come to pass. In the end I baptized thousands of pagans, including both paupers and princes. Eventually people all over Ireland converted to Christ and sent out missionaries through the whole world. Some even say that the Irish saved civilization.

Q is for quilt,
quail, and
Queen Jeanne

I ruled the quaint region of Navarre, nestled right in between the countries of Spain and France. My mom ruled before me. She became friends with Martin Luther and John Calvin. She even translated Luther's writings into French. All over France true Christians were persecuted, so I made Navarre a safe place for them to worship. I even set up schools to train pastors. My big dream was to bring the Reformation to France. But France's queen didn't want the Reformation at all. She launched a very bad time of persecution. But despite all the suffering, believers still wouldn't quit.

QUEEN JEANNE

R

R is for
rabbit, rook, and
Bishop **Ridley,**
Reformation
martyr

I was chaplain to King Henry VIII and later I was the Bishop of Rochester. I rode a horse all around the region making sure people understood the gospel and the Reformation. Next, I was Bishop of London. But then Queen Mary came to the throne and ordered me to recant my views. I refused. My friend Hugh Latimer and I were burned at the stake. Just before we died as martyrs, my friend said to me, "Be of good cheer, Master Ridley, this day we will light a candle in England that, by God's grace, will never be put out."

NICHOLAS RIDLEY

CHARLES SPURGEON

S is for
sermons, smoke, and Charles Haddon **Spurgeon**

When I was a boy I would sneak off to read books. My favorite was Bunyan's *Pilgrim's Progress.* By the time I was sixteen years old I was preaching sermons. That's no surprise, since my family is full of pastors. My dad, granddad, brothers, and even my twin sons were all preachers. So many people came to hear me preach that we built a big church called Metropolitan Tabernacle. It was in a part of the city of London called "Elephant and Castle." It was big, but not big enough for elephants! I loved to preach sermons to children. I told everyone, small and big, that we are all great sinners, but Jesus is a far greater Savior.

23

TERTULLIAN

If you think that **my** hat looks funny, then you should see what the **next** guy is wearing . . .

T is for
turban, triangle, and **Tertullian,** ancient theologian

My full name is Quintus Septimius Florens Tertullianus, but you can call me Tertullian. I was born around AD 150 in Carthage, on the northern coast of Africa. When I was really old, at age forty, I became a Christian. I quickly became a theologian, someone who studies the Bible and teaches others about God. I coined a very important term, the word "Trinity." This word means that God is one being in three persons. God is three in one. It can be tricky—but it's an important truth. I wrote many books, all devoted to pursuing the truth that is found in God's Word. Try saying this ten times: *Tertullian tells the truth.*

U is for

ukulele,
unicycle,
and
Zacharias
Ursinus

U probably don't know me. My last name means "bear," but I don't growl. I first went to school in Martin Luther's hometown. Then I went to Geneva and had John Calvin as a teacher. After all that school I went to Heidelberg. I was a teacher of theology and I was a preacher. I was very busy and never hibernated. I soon realized that many of the big ideas we talked about needed to be taught to children. So some friends and I wrote a catechism. The first question is, *What is your only comfort in life and death?* Here's the answer: *That*

I am not my own, but belong—body and soul, in life and in death—to my faithful Savior Jesus Christ. He has fully paid for all my sins with his precious blood, and has set me free from the tyranny of the devil. He also watches over me in such a way that not a hair can fall from my head without the will of my Father in heaven: in fact, all things must work together for my salvation. Because I belong to him, Christ, by his Holy Spirit, assures me of eternal life and makes me wholeheartedly willing and ready from now on to live for him. Lots of kids have memorized this. You should give it a try.

ZACHARIAS URSINUS

V is for
violin,
vanilla,
and Antonio
Vivaldi

I was born in Venice, Italy. I later moved to Vienna, surrounded by the Swiss Alps. From the time I was very young I loved music. I especially loved to play the violin. My father taught me how to play and I also taught others. My first students were girls in an orphanage. I used my gifts to sing praises to God and to write music. I wrote all kinds of music: music for the church, music about nature, and music for special events. I once wrote a very long piece of music called *The Four Seasons.* I was ordained as a priest and was called "The Red-haired Priest." Make that "The Red-haired Priest Who Could Play the Violin."

ANTONIO VIVALDI

THE WESLEYS

W is for
wig, weasel,
and John and
Charles **Wesley**

We were brothers. When we were young our house burned down and we had to jump out the windows! After growing up, we sailed over to America to work as missionaries. Later, we went back to living near Westminster and Windsor. We rode horses all over the countryside, preaching outdoors to huge crowds. We also wrote over 7,000 hymns. Charles's hymns are a little better, but Mom always said, "Boys, it's not a competition."

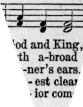

FOR A THOUSAND

ou -sand tongues to sing
- ter and my God,
e that charms our fears,
r of canceled sin,
His praise, ye dumb,

od and King,
th a-broad
-ner's ears.
- est clean
- ior com

27

FRANCIS XAVIER

X is for
xylophone,
X-ray, and
Xavier

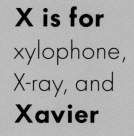

There aren't many people whose name begins with X. There's Xerxes, an ancient king of Persia, and there are a lot of cities and people in China that start with an X. Then there's me, Francis Xavier. I was named for Xavier Castle in Spain, my family's castle and the place where I was born. I wanted to be a missionary so I set sail for Asia. I worked with pearl fishermen off the coast of India. I also helped many poor children in Sri Lanka and met Samurai warriors in Japan. Since I had a hard time learning Japanese, I used paintings to teach about Christianity. My goal was to get to China, and I died in 1552 on an island just off the coast of that country.

FLORENCE YOUNG

I was born in New Zealand (and the letter "Z" comes next!). I moved with my brothers to Queensland in Australia. I taught the workers on the sugar plantations how to read the Bible. I even founded a mission called the Queensland Kanaka Mission. I met Hudson Taylor, a missionary to China. He encouraged me to go to China as a missionary. After I was there for a few years, I had to leave during the Boxer Rebellion, a time when missionaries were attacked and thrown out. But I couldn't be stopped. For the next forty years, I sailed on a yacht around the Solomon Islands dotting the South Seas. By the time I died, the South Seas Evangelical Mission church had 9,000 members. That's a lot of sailing.

Z is for
zebra, zero, and Ulrich **Zwingli,** Zurich's Reformer

I always come last because my name starts with "Z." Zurich starts with a "Z" too. God used me to teach the people of the city of Zurich about Jesus. From Zurich, the Reformation spread to other cities in Switzerland (there's a "Z" in that word, too). I preached many sermons. One of them had a funny title, "On the Choice and Freedom of Foods." In my day there were all sorts of rules that we were told we had to follow if we wanted to know Jesus. These rules served to hide the gospel. One of the rules wouldn't let us eat meat on Fridays during Lent. But my friends and I liked sausage— we were Swiss, you know. We had a sausage supper on Friday and I preached my sermon on food on Sunday. The Reformation came to Zurich. I wanted everyone to know that we should follow God's Word and do what it says. The Bible tells us everything we need to know from A to Z.

ULRICH ZWINGLI

. . . and that's church history from A to Z.

Well, at least part of it. To help fill in the picture, we've added some more information below on the people in this book, along with explanations of some of the details in the illustrations.

Augustine (354–430)

The most significant figure in the early church and maybe in all of church history, Augustine wrote *The Confessions* and the *City of God.* His writings actually fill shelves, as he kept a team of scribes busy nearly around the clock. Augustine was crucial to the formation of many doctrines, especially the doctrines of sin and salvation. From the early 400s until the end of his life he was embroiled in controversy with Pelagius. Augustine argued that we are all sinners because of Adam's fall, which is called the doctrine of original sin. God as "the Hound of Heaven" chases us down and draws us to himself. That's why God loves us before we love him.

At his death in 430, the Vandals were laying siege to Hippo, in modern day Morocco, where Augustine served as Bishop. He orchestrated the final attempts to defend the city from his deathbed. Too weak to hold his beloved books, he had his scribes write the words of the Psalms across the walls and ceiling.

Anne Bradstreet (1612–1672)

Though born in England, Anne Bradstreet is considered America's first poet. While in England, Bradstreet, then Anne Dudley, enjoyed a substantial education, largely by reading. Her father served as steward to the Earl of Lincoln, providing Bradstreet access to a massive library. She was influenced by her reading of the classical poets, as well as the poetry of John Milton. In 1628 she suffered from small pox and married Simon Bradstreet. Two years later they came to the New World with John Winthrop on the *Arbella.*

The Bradstreet family experienced all the hardships and adventures shared by the early settlers, ranging from house fires to Indian attacks. She had eight children, calling them chicks and herself a mother hen in one of her poems. "I happy am if well with you," she wrote, referring to her children. Her first book of poetry was published in 1650. Through all her poetry, Bradstreet reflected on the goodness and sovereignty of God—two pillars of Puritan belief.

John Calvin (1509–1564)

Calvin would have turned 500 in 2009 and people still talk about him. He was born in France and longed to see his native country embrace the Reformation, but he spent most of his life as a pastor in Geneva, Switzerland, just across the border. He wrote a number of books, most notably *The Institutes of the Christian Religion,* a true classic. He was married and had one son, who died as an infant.

After Calvin's death, his followers living in the Netherlands expressed his ideas in a document called the Canons of Dort, from the Synod at the city of Dordtrecht, held in 1618-1619. This document was later summarized by the acrostic T-U-L-I-P: **T** for total depravity, **U** for unconditional election, **L** for limited atonement, **I** for irresistible grace, and **P** for perseverance of the saints. Calvin's own motto has an outstretched hand offering a heart to God with the words, "My heart I offer to you, O Lord, promptly and sincerely."

John Donne (1572–1631)

John Donne was many things, including a lawyer, a politician, and a pastor. But he is best known as a poet. His *Holy Sonnets* are theologically rich poetic expressions of his love and devotion to God. In one of them he writes,

Batter my heart, three-person'd God, for you
As yet but knock, breathe, shine, and seek to mend;
That I may rise and stand, o'erthrow me, and bend
You force to break, blow, burn, and make me new.

John Donne was poised for quite a career in London politics. Then he fell in love with and married Anne More in 1601, against her father's wishes. He happened to be Lieutenant of the Tower of London and had Donne jailed for a short time, prompting Donne to write: *John Donne. Anne Donne. Un-done.* Later his father-in-law warmed up to him. John and Anne had twelve children, but five of them died before reaching adulthood. Donne also buried his wife in 1617 and never remarried.

Jonathan Edwards (1703–1758)

In 1741, during the time of the Great Awakening in the American colonies, Jonathan Ed-

wards preached what is likely the most famous sermon of all time, "Sinners in the Hands of an Angry God." In that sermon, Edwards likens sinners to spiders dangling over a pit and hanging by a mere thread of web. Edwards seemed keen on spiders, writing his first piece for publication on the flying spider.

A native of Connecticut and a graduate of Yale, Edwards spent the majority of his life in Massachusetts. He first served as pastor at Northampton from 1728 until 1750. His congregation actually voted him out. He next moved to Stockbridge, where he served among the Mohawks and Mohicans (the same tribe of *Last of the Mohicans* fame). He left in January of 1758 to become president of Princeton University. He died on March 22, 1758, from complications following a smallpox inoculation.

While Edwards gets caricatured as being mean-spirited and spewing hellfire and brimstone, the reality is his sermons and writings overflow with the words *joy, pleasure, delight,* and *enjoyment.* He enjoyed God first and foremost. He also enjoyed the world God made. He especially enjoyed cheese and chocolate, his two favorite foods. Among his many papers are receipts for pounds and pounds of chocolate he had shipped in from Boston.

John Foxe (1516–1587)

Foxe's Book of Martyrs is third in line next to the Bible and *Pilgrim's Progress* as the most beloved and read text of the church. It memorializes the martyrs down through the centuries, from the days of the apostles to persecutions under Queen Mary in the 1550s in England. John Foxe personally knew many of these martyrs and wrote his book so that the church wouldn't forget the sacrifice made by those in the previous decade and the previous centuries.

Foxe started writing on ancient Christian martyrs while at Basel, Switzerland, during his exile. When he returned to England, he was granted full access to the public records and heresy or martyrdom trial transcripts of the 1550s. When word spread of his work, people all over England sent him accounts of martyrdoms. Foxe is holding two illustrations of martyrdoms from an early edition of his book. The painting next to the F depicts the martyrdom of St. Sebastian in 288 by the Roman Emperor Diocletian.

Lady Jane Grey (1537–1554)

The Reformation began in England in 1534 under Henry VIII. During the reign of Edward VI (1547–1553), it made great strides forward, largely due to the efforts of Thomas Cranmer. Edward VI began his reign at merely nine years old. Many likened him to Israel's King Josiah. Never in good health, his reign came to an end with his death in 1553. Lady Jane Grey was not in direct line for the throne, but some leading Protestants feared what would happen if Mary, Edward VI's half-sister and a staunch Roman Catholic, would ascend the throne. Jane never had the full support she needed. Nine days after her coronation, Mary's troops routed the army, taking London and the throne. Jane was imprisoned in 1553 and put to death in 1554. She was sixteen. Mary went on to earn her reputation as the infamous "Bloody Mary."

Lady Jane Grey not only holds the record for England's shortest reign, she was also quite the theologian and quite courageous. She defended the principles of *sola Scriptura* and *sola fide*, the authority of Scripture and justification by faith alone. "Faith only in Christ's blood saves us," she said at her trial. A later descendant in her family line, the Second Earl Grey, became well known for a particular blend of tea, dubbed "Earl Grey." Rather British, eh, wot?

Hippolytus (170–236)

Hippolytus was a disciple of Irenaeus, who was bishop at Lyons in France and a disciple of Polycarp, who was an early Christian martyr and a disciple of the apostle John. Hippolytus was bishop of Rome. Actually, he was *one* of the bishops of Rome. There was a dispute there among the church and it resulted in the appointment of rival bishops. In a time of persecution, the Roman emperor exiled them both to the island of Sardinia. Hippolytus died in exile and, presumably, reconciled with Pontian, the rival bishop, just before his death.

Hippolytus wrote many books, including commentaries on the Bible and refutations of heresies, especially those denying the biblical teaching of Christ as the God-man. He also tried his hand at history, writing a complete chronology of the world from Creation until the year 234. He fell from attention until the discovery of the statue with the list of his books.

Ignatius (d.110s)

Ignatius, like the early martyr Polycarp, was also a disciple of the apostle John, linking him right to the New Testament church. He was bishop at Antioch, the place where the disciples were first called Christians (Acts 11:26).

He was summoned to Rome by the emperor Trajan. Along the way he visited with a number of Christians in various cities and wrote epistles or letters to them. In most of these letters he stresses the belief in the incarnation and in the humanity of Christ. There was a prominent heresy circulating at that time called Docetism, which held that Christ only *appeared* to be human. Ignatius countered by declaring (again and again) that Christ was really and truly human, that he really was born and lived, that he really was crucified and buried, and that he really rose again—all for us and for our salvation. When Ignatius finally made it to Rome, Trajan had him put to death.

Absalom Jones (1746–1818)

During the opening prayers of a Sunday service in 1786 at St. George's Methodist Episcopal Church in Philadelphia, ushers tapped some black worshippers on the shoulder, requesting that they move to seating designated for blacks. Two leaders of the few dozen African American worshippers led the group out of the church and eventually started new ones. The first leader, Richard Allen, a former slave, eventually formed the Bethel African Methodist Episcopal Church and the African Methodist Episcopal (AME) denomination. The second leader, Absalom Jones, also a former slave, founded the African Church of St. Thomas in the Protestant Episcopal Church.

As a young boy, Absalom Jones saved money he earned from tips as a house slave to buy a spelling book and a New Testament. He taught himself how to read. Jones loved to quote Galatians 5:1: *"Stand fast therefore in the liberty by which Christ has made us free, and do not be entangled again with a yoke of bondage."*

John Knox (c. 1514–1572)

Ordained as a Roman Catholic priest, John Knox became committed to the Protestant Reformation through the influence of George Wishart. Knox accompanied Wishart on his early travels as an armed bodyguard, which explains the knife. Knox soon became a rather energetic if not fiery preacher. He was arrested and sentenced to two years on a galley ship, then later exiled to Geneva during the reign of "Bloody Mary" in the 1550s. He wrote *The First Blast against the Monstrous Regiment of Women*, aimed at Mary. She died, though, just as the book came out. The book then rather angered Elizabeth I, whose portrait appears next to the K. Knox also had a contentious relationship with the other Mary—Mary, Queen of Scots. A leading figure in the formation of the Presbyterian Church,

Knox was central to the Reformation in Scotland. So impressed was he with Calvin's Geneva that Knox had hopes to see Scotland become a covenantal nation. His nation, however, has mostly forgotten him—a parking lot stands over his grave.

Martin Luther (1483–1546)

Martin Luther stands at the headwaters of the Reformation, which along with the Renaissance changed the entire world. Luther started out as a lawyer then became a monk. He just had too many questions and doubts about the status quo. On October 31, 1517, he nailed his Ninety-Five Theses to the church door at Wittenberg, hence the mallet in his hand. He hoped simply to start a debate. It led to much more, resulting in his break from the Catholic Church and the beginning of Protestantism.

Engraved on the head of the mallet is Luther's seal or symbol, which consists of a black cross in a red heart in a white rose against a blue sky, all enclosed by a gold circle. All of these have meaning for him. Perhaps you can do some detective work and find out why. He's also holding a lute, an early version of the guitar. Luther loved music and wrote a number of great hymns, such as "A Mighty Fortress Is Our God."

Monica (331–387)

Monica had three children, two boys and a girl. One of the boys, Augustine, is pretty famous. With a mother's pride, she's displaying his picture. Her son writes quite a bit about her in his book, *The Confessions.* He recalls how his mother never stopped praying for him, and even how she followed him around during his travels. They originally lived in North Africa, under Roman control at the time. Augustine, though, set off for Italy, ending up at the city of Milan. There Monica met up with him. Through her influence, Augustine came under the influence of Ambrose. Then, through a series of events, Augustine converted to Christianity. He immediately went to tell her about it. She offered up a prayer of thanksgiving, praising God for being "more than powerful enough to carry out all your purpose beyond all our hopes and dreams." Through all the twists and turns of her son's life, she never gave up hope and she never stopped praying for him.

John Newton (1725–1807)

John Newton's story is the story of God's amazing grace. The slave shackles point to Newton's pre-conversion life. The sheet music of "Amazing Grace" signifies his post-conversion life. Newton came under the influence of John and Charles Wesley and George Whitefield around 1755. He became an avid student of theology. By 1757 he was ready for ordination, his self-education and life experience counting as his training. His first pastorate was in Olney in southeast England. There he preached and wrote hymns, publishing *Olney Hymns* in 1779. The next year he took a pastorate in London, where he had great influence, especially over the young Member of Parliament William Wilberforce. Newton convinced Wilberforce, who thought about leaving politics for the ministry, that he could make a great contribution by working tirelessly to abolish the slave trade. Wilberforce first introduced the bill to abolish the slave trade in England in 1791. It was passed into law in 1807, just months before the death of John Newton.

John Owen (1616–1683)

Yes, it's true that oxford button-down shirts and v-neck sweaters weren't quite in style in the 1600s, but the skull cap, as Owen is wearing, was in style, and John Owen never left home—or at least never sat for a portrait—without one. Owen was a stalwart Puritan minister and theologian. He wrote extensively, including a multi-volume commentary on the book of Hebrews and numerous theological texts, such as *The Death of Death in the Death of Christ,* on the nature and extent of Christ's atonement. During the Puritan reign in England in the 1650s, Owen served as vice-chancellor of his alma mater, Oxford University, pictured in the background. In 1660, during Charles II's reign and the "Restoration," he lost his post. He took a pastorate in London where, ironically, Charles II often went to hear him preach. He's buried just a few feet away from his friend John Bunyan.

Patrick (c. 390–c. 461)

Shamrocks, wearing green, and leprechauns, not to mention the folklore of ridding all of Ireland of snakes—more myth surrounds Patrick than likely anyone else in this book. Truth be told, he wasn't even Irish. He was probably born in Wales. He has been claimed as a saint by the Roman Catholic Church and a symbol of (or excuse for) rowdy partying by others. He belongs, however, squarely as a hero for the church that desires to be faithful to Scripture and orthodox theology. He did wield massive influence over Ireland, leading to Christ nearly an entire country engrossed in the darkness of the pagan myths of the druids. He did so at the cost of great persecution and numerous attempts made on his life. He persevered, seeing his life as an act of worship in gratitude for God's saving grace. You can read his story in his autobiography, *Confessions* (c. 450). He also pops up in Thomas Cahill's best seller, *How the Irish Saved Civilization.*

Queen Jeanne of Navarre (1528–1572)

Jeanne D'Albret became ruler of Navarre in 1555. Navarre today is part of Spain, bordering France. At the time of the Reformation it was an independent kingdom aligned with France. Navarre became a sanctuary for those committed to the cause of the Reformation, called the Huguenots. Marguerite of Navarre, Jeanne's mother, began the role of Navarre as a safe haven for the Reformation. Jeanne furthered the Reformation cause in Navarre and sought to see it spread to France. She arranged for a marriage of her son that would secure him the throne of France, bringing Protestantism with him. Jeanne, however, died two months before the wedding. The Queen of France, Catherine de Medici, took advantage of the situation to keep France Roman Catholic, defaulting on the plan. On St. Bartholomew's Day, August 18, 1572, the day of the wedding, Queen Catherine authorized a widespread slaughter of Protestants. On that day in Paris alone 2,000 were martyred, most of them gathered there for the wedding. The martyrdoms continued for months.

Bishop Nicholas Ridley (1500–1555)

John Foxe tells the story of Bishop Ridley's martyrdom. He was put on trial and martyred along with Hugh Latimer, Bishop of Worcester. Both supported the crowning of Lady Jane Gray. Mary ordered them to be sent to Oxford for their trial. They were publicly burned at the stake on October 16, 1555. A cobblestone cross in the modern asphalt commemorates the spot.

Educated at Cambridge, Paris, and Louvain, Ridley was master at Pembroke College, Cambridge. Through the efforts of Thomas Cranmer, his close ally, he then served as chaplain to Henry VIII, and later was appointed bishop by Edward VI. Ridley influenced Edward VI in establishing significant works of charity. Ridley also left a mark on England's theology and worship. His work ceased with his imprisonment, but his martyrdom has made him a national hero and a significant figure in the history of the church. As an English gentleman-scholar, he most assuredly played chess, the bishop being most certainly his favorite piece.

Charles Spurgeon (1834–1892)

Charles Spurgeon grew up surrounded by pastors, the Bible, and devotional books like *The Pilgrim's Progress From This World to That Which Is to Come.* As a sixteen-year-old caught in a snowstorm, Spurgeon wandered into a Primitive Methodist Chapel on his way to a different church. The text of the sermon was Isaiah 45:22, "Turn unto me and be saved, all the ends of the earth! For I am God and there is no other." That night Spurgeon was converted and would soon be preaching with similar conviction in London pulpits. He married Susanna Thompson in 1856. They had twin sons, who both became pastors. He preached from Metropolitan Tabernacle, which seated 6,000, from 1861 until a few months before his death. He called one of his sermons "The Wordless Book." He's holding his version of three pages—black for our sin, red for Christ's atoning blood, and white for forgiveness—in his left hand. He wrote extensively and published his own magazine, *The Sword and the Trowel,* which might help to explain what he is holding in his right hand.

Tertullian (c. 160–220)

The teaching that God is three separate persons, yet one being or one substance, is all over the pages of the Bible, but it was Tertullian who coined the term "Trinity" as a quite helpful way to summarize this difficult-to-grasp concept. The painting depicts God the Father, the Holy Spirit as the dove, and Christ as the suffering Savior. Tertullian also gave us the insightful phrase, "The blood of the martyrs is the seed of the church." And he coined two other well-used terms, "Old Testament" and "New Testament."

In addition to coming up with all of these terms, Tertullian, from his post in Roman North Africa, wrote against the heresies of his day, especially those which denied the humanity of Christ. If Jesus didn't suffer as a real human, then all the suffering of the Christians under Roman rule was in vain. In fact, without a Savior who identifies with us in our humanity, Tertullian reasoned, our faith is in vain.

Zacharias Ursinus (1534–1583)

Let's explain the bear cap. Zacharias Ursinus was born Zacharias *Baer*—the German word for bear. As was the custom, when young Zacharias went off for university studies he took a Latin name. He chose Ursinus, from the Latin word for bear (think Ursinus Major, the "Big Bear" constellation). Ursinus did wear a cap, just not one with fuzzy ears. He's likely one of the least known in this book, but now you'll never forget him.

Ursinus studied at Wittenberg, Luther's city, before heading off for study at various cities in Switzerland, including John Calvin's Geneva. He then received an appointment at the rather impressive sounding Collegium Sapientiae, a seminary that was part of the University of Heidelberg in Germany. He taught everything from Aristotle to theology to Bible. He and his colleague Caspar Olevianus were the main architects of the *Heidelberg Catechism*

(1563). He spent the last three years of his life teaching at Neuchatel, Switzerland.

Antonio Vivaldi (1678–1741)

The picture in the V is of the canals of Venice, Italy, the birthplace of Antonio Vivaldi. He's far better known as a figure in music than in church history. But he was ordained and used his gifts as a violinist and composer to serve the church and to glorify God. He did indeed have red hair. He's holding sheet music from "The Four Seasons" (1723), a series of four concertos for the violin. Vivaldi cleverly has the violin and accompanying orchestra sound like spring, summer, autumn, and winter. He wrote operas, arias, concertos, and all sorts of music for the church.

His first position was Violin Maestro of the Devout Hospital of Mercy at Venice, teaching music and violin to orphaned girls. Some of the girls were then given spots in the hospital's famous orchestra and choir. Then he moved to Vienna. Much of Vivaldi's music was discovered long after he died. In fact, researchers discovered two lengthy pieces of Psalm settings in 2003 and 2005.

John Wesley (1703–1791)
Charles Wesley (1707–1788)

John and Charles had seventeen other siblings. The two traveled hundreds of thousands of miles on horseback, preached thousands of sermons to tens of thousands of people, and wrote literally thousands of hymns. Charles is pointing to one of his hymns in the picture. They grew up in an Anglican parsonage and both studied at Oxford, forming the Holiness Club with fellow member George Whitefield. They both traveled to Colonial Georgia as missionaries. And they both were converted by the words of Martin Luther (hearing them, for John, and reading them, for Charles). They both pastored churches in London, though both traveled and preached extensively. Shut out of many pulpits, they took to preaching outdoors. They were the founders of the Methodist Church. They both believed in perfectionism, or as they put it, "love perfected." John's wearing a button accordingly. And one last point for trivia: John invented an electric shock machine for the treatment of, by his count, forty-eight separate illnesses.

Francis Xavier (1506–1552)

Xavier is from the town of Xavier in Navarre, which today goes by Javier. He was born into a wealthy family, and today their castle still dominates the landscape of the town. He became a missionary, desiring to reach China. He made many lengthy stops along the way. In India his work among the poor put him at odds with the nobility. In Japan he met up with Anjiro, a nobleman quite intrigued by Xavier's mission. Anjiro supplied the Samurai warriors to escort Xavier. Xavier records that he asked Anjiro if the Japanese, who were mostly Buddhists, would become Christians. Anjiro informed him that they would first ask many questions and they would watch how Xavier lived and acted, to see if his life could back up the message. After Japan, Xavier set off for China. He made it to Shangchuan Island, China. He died just as he was planning to make the short, nine-mile trip to mainland China.

Florence Young (1856–1940)

Florence Young was born in New Zealand, but was sent back to England for boarding school. Her brothers were quite successful and she later lived with them at their sugar plantation near Queensland, Australia. She began mission work among the Kanakas, natives of the various Pacific Islands who worked the British plantations. She soon had 4,000 people attending prayer meetings. This work became the Queensland Kanakas Mission. She also went to China in the 1890s until the Boxer Rebellion, when a Chinese native group "The Righteous Fists of Harmony" launched a violent campaign against Western and Christian presence in China from 1899-1901. Many missionaries were killed, and all were forced out. Young went on to establish the South Seas Evangelical Mission, using the yacht *Evangel* to take the gospel to thousands. She wrote her autobiography *Pearls from the Pacific* in 1925. She's holding two pictures from it, one of her in native Chinese dress while there as a missionary and one of the *Evangel,* the well-traveled yacht.

Ulrich Zwingli (1484–1531)

Zwingli was one of the most colorful of a quite colorful cast of characters, the Reformers. He was trained at Basel and was there while Erasmus, the great humanist scholar, was putting together the first complete Greek New Testament. Zwingli was called to Zurich as a priest and began preaching from the Bible, starting with Matthew 1:1 on January 1, 1519. That same year, Zwingli almost died from the plague. He prayed, "In the Midst of illness, console me, Lord God." He recovered and kept preaching, which led him to many discoveries and prompted the sausage supper, which led to the sermon on the freedom of food, which led to the Reformation coming to Zurich. He died on a battlefield on October 11, 1531, while serving as a chaplain. A statue of him was erected at Zurich, with a Bible open to Matthew 11, which has the words:

"Come to me, all who labor and are heavy laden, and I will give you rest . . . For my yoke is easy and my burden is light."

I to Y?
Timeline

Alphabetical order is a great thing, but some might find it helpful to see the people in this book in *chronological order*, to get a better sense of the flow of church history:

Ignatius (d.110s)
Tertullian (c.160–220)
Hippolytus (170–236)
Monica (331–387)
Augustine (354–430)
Patrick (c. 390–c. 461)
Martin Luther (1483–1546)
Ulrich Zwingli (1484–1531)
Nicholas Ridley (1500–1555)
Francis Xavier (1506–1552)
John Calvin (1509–1564)
John Knox (c. 1514–1572)
John Foxe (1516–1587)
Queen Jeanne (1528–1572)
Zacharias Ursinus (1534–1583)
Lady Jane Grey (1537–1554)
John Donne (1572–1631)
Anne Bradstreet (1612–1672)
John Owen (1616–1683)
Antonio Vivaldi (1678–1741)
Jonathan Edwards (1703–1758)
John Wesley (1703–1791)
Charles Wesley (1707–1788)
John Newton (1725–1807)
Absalom Jones (1746–1818)
Charles Spurgeon (1834–1892)
Florence Young (1856–1940)

And don't forget . . . the story of church history is **your story!**